# WISDOM OF THE HEART

# WISDOM OF THE HEART

## Create Your Own Reality

### Ed Scott

iUniverse, Inc.

New York  Bloomington  Shanghai

**Wisdom of the Heart**

Create Your Own Reality

iUniverse books may be ordered through booksellers or by contacting:

iUniverse
1663 Liberty Drive
Bloomington, IN 47403
www.iuniverse.com
1-800-Authors (1-800-288-4677)

ISBN: 978-0-595-51436-6 (pbk)
ISBN: 978-0-595-50449-7 (cloth)
ISBN: 978-0-595-61899-6 (ebk)

Printed in the United States of America

# CONTENTS

# Preface

In publishing this book, I hope to share with you the knowledge and the opportunity to create exciting and rewarding life experiences and invite you to explore the source of your own truth and your beliefs. This begins with a raised awareness that may lead to knowledge, wisdom, and the understanding of how your beliefs are truly your biology and your destiny.

*The love and beauty that now we see:*
*This, the ultimate truth will be.*

—Ed Scott

# Introduction

This book came into being by way of very unusual circumstances. In February of 2007, I visited a psychic energy healer, to obtain an assessment of my physical condition and a healing session. A stroke had left me partially paralyzed and with impaired vision for the previous seven years. Imagine my surprise when the energy healer assessed my condition, gave me his "blessing," and then told me to get that *book* out of my head. At that instant, I saw a book cover, a book title, and some of the chapters in my mind. This energy healer went on to say that I was about to begin a new and exciting phase of my life and that I was to share my experiences and the information that was now streaming into my conscious awareness. I protested and advised him that I was now retired after thirty-six years as a police officer and that I was not a writer. He explained that, oftentimes, the human body and con- sciousness compensate for a physical dis- ability, particularly in older individuals after they have slowed their pace in life. The psychic healer further reminded me that I would know the source of the infor- mation which was coming, but would be unable to reference or document some of it. He suggested that I enjoy the experience without thinking about it too much.

For the next fourteen months, information for this book would come into my awareness when I least expected it to do so. Usually, this would occur when I was very relaxed and accepting, and in a mental state of simply *being*. As I began to write about this experience, I found that the words would come to me without any prior organized thought. Knowledge that I had learned over the past years was integrated with the new material, and I wrote the book in a conversational style. More coincidence then brought me unexpectedly to the publishing process. I hope that you will enjoy reading of a differing perspective or approach to spiritual growth.

*Wisdom of the heart* is the deep understanding and insight learned from our most memorable events, our most emotional times, and our closest personal relationships. These emotional experiences of the heart—often described as *heartfelt*, *heartwarming*, *heartbroken*, or *from the heart*—are the source of our greatest joy and our deepest sorrow. In creating our own reality, it is our human awareness and our level of consciousness that determine the nature of all realms of our experience. While many people continue to seek a spiritual experience, others have come to know that we are spiritual beings engaged in the human experience. In this age of spiritual awakening, we should look to love and to beauty in sharing the human experience with others, heart to heart.

# DESTINY ON A DVD

Years ago, a young police officer sat in the street at an accident scene, holding a dying five-year-old boy in his arms and wondering how a merciful God could allow this death to happen. A year later, the officer's firstborn son died in infancy, and still he asked, "What have I done to deserve this? And why was a baby's life abandoned?" Three years later, yet another son died a week after birth. Finally, he realized that sometimes the lessons come hard and are repeated until they are learned. Who was this man to question a divine plan for us? To the extent that he could know love, so, too, was the depth of his sorrow. It is love that allows sorrow to bring us to understanding and wisdom.

It seems obvious that the direction of our lives and the events that shape our beliefs might first depend upon our prevailing attitudes and upon our willingness to accept change. When we see this, we discover that our life's events may be shaping our beliefs, if this is what we wish to accept. More importantly, the reverse is also true: Our beliefs actually shape our life events, our destinies.

Ask yourself, "What is it that I want most in life? Do I know what is important to me in this life?" Have you ever closely examined your beliefs? Do your beliefs include resolution of questions such as: "What can I expect in another realm after death in this life? Do we retain our human awareness while transitioning to another state of being? What can I do to improve my relationships, my health, and even my financial security? Do I have the creative power to effect change? What are my intentions and purpose?" To create our reality, or to change it, we must first know our selves and our beliefs. To know our selves is to realize our true beings—not our physical bodies, not our egos, and certainly not our reputations with others. To create our reality is to change our state of being. One of the most important lessons that we can learn from experience is that our physical existence and all other realms of consciousness are simply a "state of being." All of our experiences in this physical body, and our experiences of the mind and beyond, are experienced as temporary states of being in human consciousness. Our states of being are wholly dependent upon our expanded awareness and our level of collective consciousness. For example, that which we believe about our present existence and other levels of awareness will cause things to be just as we expect. It is imperative that we increase our awareness and our consciousness. There are many paths and methods, but the surest way to examine and know our beliefs is to go within ourselves in meditation or contemplation. First, let us come to know ourselves, and then ask others for any additional knowledge or assistance. Humility should keep us from worrying about our levels of spiritual development. If we think that we are advanced or enlightened, then we are not.

Our universe is in constant evolution, and so it is with the human condition. For many years now, people around this earth have observed a remarkable and growing spiritual awakening. There appears to be a changing of a global spiritual axis from east to west. The long-held spiritual beliefs, customs, and practices of developing Asia and India appear to be dissolving, to be replaced with a more materialistic or commercial creed, while in America, our way of life is slowly evolving to embrace an increased spiritual renaissance. Our daily news informs us of growing Asian and Indian economies, increased demands from them for world resources, and changing lifestyles from poverty to an increased personal prosperity. Many developing nations seem to be more interested in acquiring nuclear weapons, political power, and international status than in emphasizing age-old customs and traditions of personal and spiritual value. In this country, many individuals and entire families have abandoned their traditional churches because of sexual abuse of children by the clergy, and church politics; they have adopted the cafeteria-style selection of a church that suits their particular beliefs. Many more have left traditional church memberships, because they have not found definitive or profound answers to substantiate their intuitive and core beliefs. There are now numerous books and other materials available regarding an intention-driven life, living deliberately with purpose, and many other approaches to personal and spiritual growth. People are now seeking answers to the many questions in their unfulfilled lives. Change usually begins with a deep sense of longing, or a wish for something unknown or missing. That longing of our souls for something more in life will prompt the search, and begin the coincidental events, that will change our lives and our consciousness in epic proportion.

Many people believe that they were born into a life experience preordained, much like a DVD movie. While some believe that we select our own human roles, others continue to believe that their predetermined role was of God's choice or simply that of coincidence. Whatever your belief, consider that even a predetermined role for your life might also include the coincidental opportunity to gain the knowledge and the capacity to change your beliefs, your present lifestyle, and your future.

Stop here and think for a moment: Are you coasting through life wondering what will come to your experience to be dealt with? Know that the reverse can be true for you. *Your beliefs create your experiences in this life!* Life comes at us fast. Most people are simply too busy with life's demanding schedules to take the time to examine their deepest longings, their worst fears, and to make a commitment to their own comforts. In 1943, noted psychologist Abraham Maslow developed his theory of human needs and motivation. He described the theory as resembling a pyramid with five ascending levels. The larger, base level was that of the basic, essential needs of food, shelter, and physical comfort. The second level was that of physical and psychological safety and security. A third, smaller level included the need for love and relationships. Higher still, the fourth level listed respect, self-esteem and prestige with recognition from others. The pinnacle or highest level of the pyramid describes the human need of self-fulfillment and self-actualization; to realize one's full potential. Perhaps it's time to maximize your awareness and knowledge of yourself beyond the Maslow-theory basics of comfort and physical needs. Self-realization should be our goal, no matter how we describe it for ourselves. Self-actualization may be pursued and obtained at any age—but first we must know ourselves: our beliefs, values, attitudes, and what it is that we desire most in life. There is magic in the creative force of this universe that can provide everything we need and those things that we ask for. Hopefully, we prefer love, compassion, beauty, joy, and understanding above the physical aspects of financial wealth and other material goods, properties, and their mental attachments. Our physical material possessions cannot define who we really are. We came into this life without possessions and will certainly leave without them. It is time we learn to see—not with our eyes, but with our hearts and our souls.

Wisdom of the heart asks that we look to those past experiences that have provided us the cherished moments, emotions, knowledge, and understanding that have contributed to our growth and innate wisdom. Most often, our memorable experiences have involved our loved ones and events that caused us an emotional experience that changed our attitudes, our values, and our understanding of things. Whether it was sorrow or joy, it was love that formed the basis for our sense of loss, pain, grief, joy, beauty, and peace. Our emotional satisfaction, our physical health and comfort, and any other valued aspect of our existence can be realized once we take the time to examine our needs and make the commitment to any necessary changes. Tragically, there are those who feel that they are victims of their environment. My heart goes out to them. When people are victimized by physical or sexual abuse, or by society, or they are traumatized by business or corporate decisions, they can become resigned to accepting these conditions as their roles. Hopefully, they will be made aware that they are people of worth and will recognize their true being as spiritual, and perfect in nature. Professional intervention services should certainly be the starting point for some who believe that they are trapped in the role of victim. All of those with a victim mentality should look closely at their beliefs and decide what is most important to them. Only then will they find the necessary change of lifestyles.

We are fortunate to live in an age of increasingly improved technology, sophisticated sciences, and nearly unlimited informational resources. It is also a time when increasing numbers of people are searching for something more meaningful in their lives. Hopefully, they will come to value most those matters of the heart that provide a sense of fulfillment and joy.

# Imagination and Consciousness

To better know our beliefs and our present orientation with regard to a collective knowledge and wisdom, it will help to examine our understanding of human awareness and consciousness. The basic elements related to human consciousness are our attention, awareness, imagination, and consciousness. Attention is best described as the probe of our awareness.

For example, your attention at this moment is directed to these words before you, yet you are simultaneously aware of the little voice in your head and the fact that you are reading these words. Many external sights, sounds, scents, and other things can also attract and hold your attention without your intention to have them do so.

The most important element of human consciousness is that of our awareness. Human awareness is simply our mental capacity of having perception, cognition, a certain knowledge, and memory. This human awareness allows us to be cognizant of our immediate thoughts and the sensations received through our five senses. Our capacity for memory also allows us to be aware of past experiences.

It becomes evident, then, that human awareness gathers and collects knowledge from our experiences and stores the knowledge both in our conscious and our subconscious mind. Our consciousness also provides additional levels of mental and spiritual experiences with more knowledge. For most of us, human consciousness is largely unexplored and our subconscious minds are not accessible without medical or psychiatric assistance. The whole of our human consciousness includes the larger area of subconsciousness that is more often described as our *superconsciousness*. Our superconsciousness also controls and maintains our body's autonomic systems. We humans consciously utilize but a small amount of our brain capacities, and the vast majority of us have not yet considered using the human mind to further develop our awareness to expand our consciousness.

Human intuition is another phenomenon of consciousness that is often misunderstood. Many books and writings are available offering help in developing our intuition. However, it has been my experience that intuition cannot be developed. Intuition is simply there. Only our *awareness* and *recognition* of the intuitive thought and our responses to it can be developed. Intuition arises from the subconscious level of our minds to a cognitive level of consciousness—much like our voice of conscience telling us that something is amiss or that something exists and is correct. It is the rational, thinking analysis of the mind that will then alter or destroy the original intuitive message that came to us without any thought. Many law enforcement officers have found that their intuition has served them well, guiding them to be in the right place at the right time, and saving them from serious physical harm in a violent environment. Imagine an officer entering a dark warehouse, intuitively sensing a hidden threat, and requesting a canine team to search for an armed intruder. Many people have experienced an incident where intuition has caused them to know when others were being untruthful. The key to using our intuition is to learn to recognize our instinctive, intuitive feelings and to trust these feelings without ignoring or destroying them with the ego. For example, when reading this book, you might instantly recognize a bit of information that you intuitively know to be true, without having previously thought about it. Most of our intuitive feelings are of a positive nature. For example, most of us can remember meeting a stranger for the first time and having a natural hunch or gut feeling, an immediate rapport with this person. There is also a direct relationship of human intuition with coincidence. When we are presented with a coincidence or a series of coincidences, it is our intuition that first brings our awareness into focus. Incredibly, after we recognize the synchronicity of coincidental events, more coincidence will follow, when we learn to trust and follow these unscheduled or unexpected events.

Another important element of the functions of our minds and our consciousness is that of our human imagination. While random sights and sounds can capture our attention, our imagination is far more capable, in that it can create sights, sounds, and experiences on which to direct and focus our attention. For example, if I suggest to you that you picture an angel in your mind, you can readily see the angel in your imagination. We all use the creative power of imagination for planning our vacations, preparing for a dinner party, and anticipating most of our everyday experiences.

The wonderful thing about imagination is that once you begin to direct and control it, the imagination expands and becomes unlimited. It is only then that we tap into the unseen powers of this universe. The most successful people, whom we have remembered throughout history, have had vision—they have used their imaginations for great things. They did not believe anything to be a "stretch of the imagination." The least that we can do for ourselves and others is to begin to imagine a wondrously happy and successful life. Imagine it, and it can come true! Believe it, and it will happen. As we think and believe, so we shall become. Where attention goes, energy flows.

Many people believe that our consciousness is "just there" and that we cannot change our consciousness. It is important to know that we can alter or raise our own consciousness. When we are coasting along without control, our consciousness will create and influence our life experiences. Just imagine now how haphazard our lives would be if experiences that are stored in consciousness were retrieved to create more of the same kinds of random, unwanted, or unhealthy experience.

Psychology defines consciousness as having thought, cognition, volition or will power, emotion, and sensation. These elements allow us to change or expand our consciousness, so why not take control and create the experiences that we wish for and gain the wisdom of the heart? The real you, the soul, the silent listener can silence the egoistic mind and look at consciousness to realize what has been happening to your life.

Centuries ago, a French philosopher altered history when he postulated a theory of human existence. Descartes then wrote, "I think, therefore I am," believing that because of the capacity of his mind to think with cognition, that he must therefore exist. Was Descartes not aware of his awareness? Too bad that Descartes did not know more of his ego, consciousness, and the fact that he was only partially correct in describing his own unlimited power of beliefs and human consciousness. Perhaps he did know, but lacked the vocabulary or literary tools of today to fully express himself. It is also likely that the world was not yet ready for Descartes' insight.

Once we are aware that our beliefs can determine our future life experiences, we can take that responsibility and that opportunity to insist upon positively projected life experiences, rather than waiting for life to provide us with a randomly, repeated experience with limited learning and knowledge. Create your reality and determine your future.

A point of clarification is needed regarding my use of the word *coincidence* in this writing. The word coincidence is used simply as a conversational convenience to describe the synchronicity of unexpected and unique occurrences. Many would say that there is no such thing as a coincidence, as all events or happenings were preordained as necessary for the overall integration of our affairs.

# ALL IN THE UNIVERSE IS ENERGY

Our elegant universe contains everything we need to know in order to acquire peace, joy, love, beauty, health, wealth, knowledge, and spiritual awakening. There are many unseen, not yet fully understood, forces and powers in our universe that can enable us to raise our awareness and consciousness to our full potential. How we define for ourselves our purpose in life will also define how we begin to use the creative powers available.

The science of physics proposes that everything in our physical universe consists of vibratory energy. Light, sound, solids, liquids, body tissue—all things—are comprised of energy. Science has further demonstrated that energy is often transferred or changed, but never lost. The unseen energies produced by our concentrated thoughts are very powerful and are not without consequence. Notable scientist Albert Einstein once declared that the nature of any lab experiment is influenced by the person conducting the experiment, simply due to the energy transmitted by the thoughts and visual concentration of the scientist. Our thoughts leave our minds as energy forms, whether the thoughts are positive, negative, or neutral. Thought energy may also be directed, and this energy, too, is never lost. When we think negative thoughts, this energy will not only return to us, but will attract more of the same negative energy to us. A scientific principle postulates that at the level of vibratory string theory, energy attracts similar or same energy. At a gross lower vibratory energy level, opposites attract and entrain one another, much as magnets do. *We have been attracting our life events with our thought energies.* Our lives today are exactly what we have thought about in past years, and our lives tomorrow are determined by what we think and believe today.

Because the laws of nature and physics are immutable, they are also predictable.

Those things that mean the most to us and truly warm our hearts are available to anyone who understands that we do create our own reality—and who also has the courage to seek change. Many of us have already changed our lives with a positive mental outlook. By way of faith and our beliefs, we were then fortunate to discover our inner being, or consciousness, and know the difference between *being* and *thinking*. Probably the majority of people worldwide continue to wonder why they were given such intolerable bad luck in this physical existence. It isn't a matter of luck.

Earlier, I mentioned that our beliefs regarding all realms of our consciousness are dependent upon our awareness, perception, and our knowledge. Many people

talk of "going home" when this life is fin-
ished. The words may sound poetic or
soothing, but they are not accurate. The
truth is that we don't go anywhere in the
physical sense, but our consciousness then
enters a state of being that shows us that
we have been freed to return to our source.
We come to know that this physical existence was only a temporary stay. When our
physical bodies die and the mind no
longer functions, our soul, or consciousness, continues to exist as an energy form
or pattern in another state of being. Not
only is this life what we make of it, so is
our existence in other realms. These other
realms of possibilities are within us even
now. Those who have passed on before us
have left their energy form in the next
realm, the astral level, where their lives

and energy footprints are left in the *Akashic records*, much like a holographic record. When they died, their entire lives did come before them for review, not in a "flash" of time, but as instant knowledge. At this realm, information and experience are without phonetic words as we know them, and the receipt of information is better known as instant knowledge, with a full and complete understanding. The instant review of our lives provides a complete understanding of the pain or harm we may have caused others and the role of love and beauty in our existence.

In the next chapter, I will present a larger concept that can have a profound effect upon our lives. This requires an understanding of how we create our reality as a *state of being*, not only in this physical and emotional-mental existence, but also in all other realms of our consciousness.

# THE SECRET OF THE ANCIENTS

There is a secret esoteric knowledge that has been passed down through the ages, which has empowered people the world over to become successful in their personal endeavors—these could be financial wealth, health, knowledge, comfort, relationships, job performance, or numerous other areas. Many people have found a secret creative force of the universe and

have used this knowledge for many pur-
poses. We can use this secret knowledge to
change our lives or create a new reality.
Conversely, we may have to change our
beliefs to access and use the secret knowledge.

Historically, religious scripture, text, and
policies have made reference to a secret
knowledge, but many of these have been
changed and rewritten. These scriptures
and texts have been passed along to the
faithful only after being subjected to interpretation by religious leaders. Many original scriptures and texts available still
contain words, phrases, and references
written in an esoteric manner, which
remain unknown to the average reader.
For example, the words, "Ask of this in my
name and you shall receive," do not fully

detail just what was originally meant. How about the words, "The kingdom of heaven is within"? How many of the religious population have looked beyond the human ego and beyond the words to apply this knowledge and know that this requires that we go within ourselves in meditation, in prayer, or in contemplation? The same secret knowledge contained in the eastern Sikh tradition of *Radha Soami* also remands the follower to go within the self with the guidance of the Master. The secrets are not secrets to those who search beyond the egoistic exercises of reading, research, and discussion.

Over centuries, the search for answers and the study of human spirituality has evolved considerably. Beginning with the mass subscription to religious codes of ethics from the church, mosque, or synagogue, the search has come beyond a new-age, drug-induced awareness. Today, the studies of human consciousness and spirituality are reinforced by science and quantum physics. No matter what changes occur in society and our contemporary fads, the ancient secret knowledge remains unchanged. We, the searchers, have also evolved sufficiently to better recognize the meaning and the implications of the secret teachings.

To take advantage of the secret knowledge, we must follow very specific rules. To access the knowledge available, we must first approach life with positive and open minds and hearts. Our request for mental and material things must be worded very precisely and in a positive manner. We cannot ask for something not to occur or ask anything injurious to others. For example, we cannot ask for a better life, as this implies the negative element that says we presently have an undesirable or unwanted life. The negative aspect of this position will only attract more of the same for our lives. We can begin by realizing that we already have a good life, are grateful for this, and that we simply wish to make changes.

Secondly, our request for something should be reasonable, and we must believe with total faith that it will happen as a matter of absolute law. We will not know the timing of the occurrence for our request, any more than we can possibly know of the intricate, interwoven coincidence required to make it happen. We must not even think about how it will occur, as our doubts will overcome our faith and negate the request. To expedite our requests, we will almost always be required to make a minimal physical effort to obtain results. For example, if you ask for a new motor vehicle, you probably should promptly answer the sweepstakes entry when it arrives in the mail. Many of us have enjoyed using this knowledge in our daily affairs without consciously knowing what it was that worked so well. For many years, I believed that I lived a charmed life, or that it was the gift of grace from a nameless god. Now that I know how the secret knowledge works, with my submission to a greater, creative force, my life has changed considerably. Recently, I asked for help in making a decision regarding our older car: Should we repair the high-mileage car or trade up for a newer model? In my mind, I visualized a larger, newer model with comfortable seating and electronic dash instruments. As I imagined myself behind the steering wheel, the car appeared as silver colored with gray interior. In less than a week, an auto sales person phoned to suggest that our car, with its high mileage, was probably now requiring repairs. She asked if we would like to test-drive a newer model. The coincidences were now beginning to make sense. My wife and I visited the sales lot and viewed several newer-model cars. We decided that the new models were not the type of car that we wished to purchase. Upon turning to leave the sales lot, we found a newer silver

Buick blocking our exit. This car was a late-model trade-in with very low miles and was listed in Consumer Reports as a "best buy." To make a long story shorter: We were given a trade-in value of more than twice what we anticipated, and the new Buick was significantly reduced with a sale price. Exactly as I had envisioned, the interior color of the car was gray, and it had total electronic or digital instrumentation with diagnostics included and comfortable, adjustable power seats! We only had to follow the numerous coincidences to find a new car and enjoy a savings of several thousand dollars. There are numerous other times when I have asked for help with an anticipated problem and found that a simple solution was then presented to me, or that someone else had unexpectedly volunteered to help and solved my problem. After that, I concentrated on asking, "What can I do for others and to improve relationships?" The next thing I knew, I was writing a book. Whenever we ask for something that benefits others or is for the good of the entire planet, the response can be very powerful and far-reaching. Be careful what you ask for, and always say thank-you. Gratitude is key.

A simple way to put this knowledge to work for us is to begin and end each day with a thankful acknowledgement of our present life situation. We can also request a visible sign that we are going to experience a beautiful day—safe, and with positive experiences in doing what is right. Others may say that this is living in God's will. We still continue to plan our necessary daily activities, but now enjoy each and every hour of the day. When we anticipate a difficult or strenuous task, we can simply ask for help. We can do so silently or audibly. Some will call this prayer. You needn't be surprised when friends appear unexpectedly to help. Even when a seemingly tragic event occurs, we can begin to see it as living in the Creator's will, as a matter for our acceptance, learning, and understanding. Those of us who have difficulty with the word *God* can substitute titles of: Creator, Supreme Being, Lord, universe, world of coincidence, or anything we wish. Our faith, sincerity, acceptance, and gratitude will speed the arrival of information, events, coincidence, and even material objects in accordance with our requests. The most rewarding of these, however, are those things, not of a physical property, but those of the heart. Many will say that it is because we are living in God's will, or the laws of the universe, and that ours is the gift of grace.

Remember that wisdom of the heart is the deep understanding and insight learned from our most cherished, memorable, and emotional events. These emotion-filled memories are most likely the end result of love, joy, beauty, sorrow, or suffering. Unfortunately, we remember some of our past experiences because they made us fearful. These, too, became etched in our consciousness and brought back to our awareness. We need to learn to meet fear head-on and look closely at the root cause and the lack of knowledge about the cause. Understanding will erase fear. As our awareness and consciousness grows, so too will our wisdom. Fear is a product of the ego and is the opposite of love. Fear destroys faith. We must learn to live fearlessly. Everything works out just the way it is supposed to, even if it works out differently than we had hoped or planned.

Now, let's concentrate on those things that we wish for in life. Remember that negative energy attracts more negative energy, and positive thoughts cause positive energies to be drawn to us. Whatever our spiritual or religious orientation, we can change our lives, change our realities, and begin to create positive changes and rewarding experiences in accordance with a greater purpose in life.

# Masters, Mystics, and Messengers

Considering what we know of the physics of energy and the impact of our beliefs and thought processes, it behooves us to see things in a positive way. In your mind, draw a line between yesterday and today. Decide that, from today forward, you will create change, and know that you are no longer bound to any negative influences: past, present, or future. When you want more positive experiences to be your future, ask for them.

Medical science has shown that our human body cells have both a basic intelligence and memory. The medical community is only now awakening to a new realm of research in the causation and treatment of our human biology. The alternative medicine professionals are working more with energy healing. All of our cells communicate with one another, as necessary to function. Consider that our cellular bodies are listening to our minds and to our thoughts. The biology of the human body includes more than fifty billion cells, and the energy of human thought has the greatest influence upon our cells. If we stand before a mirror, look at our bodies, and make negative comments, we are affecting the body experiment, and what we believe *will* attract more of the same. The case in point is the hypochondriac. He thinks of himself as suffering, believes it to be true, and wonders why he is often ill. For those who use the phrase "I'm sick and tired" of such and such, it becomes more than just a poor choice of words. Our bodies listen and react to our words, our thoughts, and our deepest beliefs, whether they are spoken or not. If we habitually think or say "sick and tired," we will likely become so. As we think and believe, so shall we become!

Other areas of negative influence are our environment and our perception of events. For example, it might be helpful to reduce our exposure to negative media reporting of news events. Very much like watching a movie, we can easily get caught up in the emotions of events and the power of words that we see and hear on our televisions and Internet sites. We should be informed, but watch a minimum of news reporting with a detached, neutral view of someone else's perspective of worldly problems. The same can be said of very negative people and environments. We can reduce our exposure and try not to get caught up in making judgments of others or speaking unkindly of them. Why let others rent that space in our heads?

For many of us, meditation and introspection serve to quiet the chattering mind and shut off events and stresses of the typical workday. With practice, a deeper level of meditation can bring us to other levels of our consciousness, which can provide experiential knowledge with understanding and answers to our many questions. At this deeper level of self-exploration, it becomes clear to us the all-important role that love and beauty play in all of creation and in all that we see, think, and do. The essence of our soul is beauty, joy, and love.

A beautiful sequence or cascade begins the moment we begin to plan our days, experiences, and our lives based upon our beliefs. The more familiar we become with this practice, the more successful it becomes. Needless to say, the more successful we then become in all of our endeavors, the more we trust and believe in coincidence, and the more often coincidence will occur for us. We can learn to see beauty and purpose in all things. The more we love, the more we become loved by others. All of our relationships will grow and become truly heart-warming, and our experiences will become treasured memories.

Once we begin our search for that which is missing in our lives, coincidence will bring us the needed resources at the precise time that we need them. This might be as simple as finding a book on the study of Eastern philosophy, or the appearance of a person who can provide us with guidance and a shared experience and knowledge. We can develop our awareness to the point that we recognize the choices and events that have come to us via coincidence.

Over the course of many years, religious figures have provided guidance with both the spoken word and writings. Various titles were bestowed upon these persons, such as Lord, master, prophet, guru, mystic, messenger, and many more. Today, we must recognize the coincidence that brings such a teacher into our lives and address these persons as they wish to be called. If you were to ask an enlightened messenger, "Who are you?" he or she would likely reply, "I am who you think I am."

In creating their own realities, many people have come to depend upon guardian angels, inner guides, and even a higher self for guidance. If there is a higher self, another entity within the self, it will likely be the human ego talking. It is my belief that these are constructs of the mind and will not provide us with guidance or dependable messages for our spiritual growth. More likely, these creations of the mind will impede our search. It helps to remember that the real *you* is the silent listener: pure awareness and consciousness. It is the human ego that speaks so loudly and so persistently through the voice in our heads that pretends to be us. Listen closely to the voice that shouts, "I am; I am all these things; I am this and that." The human ego is without a doubt the biggest obstacle to our realization of our true identity and to our spiritual growth. When we listen and become aware of the ego speaking in our heads, we quickly realize that the ego is never satisfied. Our ego demands more and more to support its own identity. Acknowledge, then, the necessity and the usefulness of the ego in doing things and the difference in our true identity of simply *being*.

*The unchanging ultimate truth is that of love and beauty.* This should be the message, no matter what the messenger is titled or called by others. The master, mystic, prophet, or messenger is not responsible for your actions, your karma, or your life—you are! Furthermore, the messenger does not create your reality—you do!

# If You Love Them,
# Tell Them So

Once love finds us worthy, it continues to grow far beyond individual relationships. We find that we will become aware that we really do love all of creation, even if we don't always understand the complexity and interrelationships involved.

Are we all really connected to one another? Yes, as bodies of energy we are connected and interact with all elements of our physical universe. We have developed relationships with family and friends, with each individual relationship formed on a different level of affection. Imagine how good it would be to get to know everyone in our lives at a deep, intimate level with an increased mutual understanding. A remarkable thing happens when, finally, we come to the point where we love all people. This point comes quickly once we begin to see others on an individual, personal level, much as we see family members. Our developed human awareness should include an acute awareness of each and every person on an individual basis.

What is it that happens when passing strangers return our smiles? Are we really strangers? What is it that we have in common? The ancient Greeks had a word for this: *philos*, meaning "brotherly love." A pleasant and welcome thing now happens to me occasionally when I am attending a public event or when I'm sitting in a restaurant. A stranger's eyes will meet mine, and this unknown person will smile, nod to me, and say hello. Age, race, and gender do not matter. Sometimes there are not words to describe the bond felt with others who we do not really know, as well as those we *do* know and love. Why not, then, begin by trying to better know those persons thought to be close to us? Do we afford them enough of our time to really listen to them with interest? Do we truly care and withhold making judgments? Do we interact with others in a guarded mode to protect ourselves, or do we meet others with love? This is only the beginning of love's communications.

When is the last time that you sat and looked directly into another's eyes while conversing, or even while remaining silent? This can be so powerful that many people cannot tolerate or handle the energy exchange. Perhaps these people cannot afford the personal honesty required. More likely they are seeing others from a cautious or guarded position. There is obviously more to communications than words alone when we want to provoke love, affection, empathy, understanding, and compassion.

It is easy to say "I love you" to family members, but why not say the same words to close friends as they leave your home after a visit? It seems that men, in particular, have a difficult time saying "I love you" to others, especially other men. Many would say that it is a cultural thing. Whose culture? All of us should be confident enough in our true identity and image to be able to show sensitivity and say what we think and feel. If our *intention of thought* toward others is accepting and loving, it will show in our energy fields, just as it will show if we greet others with cautious reserve or hostility.

Should we deny our children the pleasure and reassurance of hearing and knowing that they are loved? Even more importantly, we must share our beliefs with our children, and show them the resources available to further expand their spiritual awareness. Children live what they learn, and they learn what they live. It is not enough to raise our children in the same way that we were raised, because of the rapid acceleration of growth in today's children. Children begin to form their beliefs and behaviors even prior to their birth. We should afford them the opportunity to realize their innermost and highest potential to a level far above that which took us, as adults, many years to realize. Can you imagine what this will do to facilitate a global spiritual awakening and awareness? Our children are the future of our communities and our world. In raising our children, we provide them with advice, guidance, and an example to follow, and, for a while, they will emulate us. Not many parents or persons responsible for nurturing children consider that the actions and words they bring to a child's awareness then enter the child's memory and consciousness. Imagine the consequence of one word or action that is less than true, kind, and loving to a child developing his or her beliefs and behaviors. Children can readily observe our subtle, intentional energy displays far beyond the spoken word.

There are words sharper than a razor's edge, which need not be spoken at all. It has been said that ninety-five percent of the world's problems are the result of poor relationships—whether personal, family, community, business, governmental, or global. Even our national marriage divorce rate now exceeds fifty percent. What would our world be like if we all spoke from loving hearts and minds using clear, honest communications? Our developed languages allow for the inflection of human emotion into our words to show intent and passion, but the problems arise when other factors enter into our communications. Our perception, judgment, and preconceived beliefs too often cause us not to hear what is communicated to us by others. This can be further complicated by a lack of clarity in some spoken messages, leaving them open for interpretation.

Too often, people decide not to love another person because of this person's behavior. It appears that love is often a victim of a mental judgment. If we were all made in the image of God, shouldn't we love one another for who we are and not for what we do? It may be very difficult to love a terrorist because of his or her behavior, but let's take the time to imagine the conditions, environment, and influences that led a terrorist to his or her role in our creation. The terrorist may be thinking that we are certifiably crazy and that he or she is simply a freedom fighter. Without making a judgment, we might consider the karmic role of this freedom fighter in our reality and the possibility that a lesson is being brought to us. Are our hearts and minds open, receptive, patient, and understanding? We probably won't meet many terrorists, but we do interact with many and varied individuals. Some will always appear to be thoughtless, irrational, violent, or just plain crazy by our mental standards, but all have their own role in bringing coincidence and another lesson to others. An Oriental proverb advises us to welcome all, including strangers, as cherished and dignified guests.

In addition to loving words and sharp, unkind words, the lack or absence of words can also cause heartache. We have all lost loved ones because of accident, illness, or age. Have you ever wished that you might have said something to these people before they departed this earthly realm? For many of us, this has caused a deep sense of regret and the feeling that our relationship was unfinished, incomplete. Perhaps it was so for the person departed, as well. Consider, right now: If you knew that you were going to die in less than twenty-four hours, what would you wish to say to family members and friends to complete a mutual knowledge, understanding, and loving relationship?

Think of each of those people dearest to you and what has been taken for granted or left unsaid with them. Once we have gone on, or they have passed on, it may be too late to share what might have been needed by both of you. Why leave unsaid and unfinished those loving, kind words of appreciation, forgiveness, and affection?

# Life, Love, and Laughter

Love begets love. Remarkable changes begin to occur immediately when we change our criteria for our life experiences. Only the human mind and ego can deter love's course.

A Buddhist tradition provides a few basic keys to love and perhaps a lesson that we may consider for integration as we create new beliefs and a new reality. The first key is a loving-kindness. Even if at first we cannot feel loving toward others, we can learn to show kindness to all, and love will follow.

The second aspect is that of joy. We must fully appreciate joy when it comes and learn to find happiness in all things at all times. It's not so easy when we are fearful, uncertain, or upset, but, with practice, we can eliminate fear and doubt and learn to be comfortable with unexpected surprises, fear, loss, and other unsettling emotions.

A third aspect is that of compassion. Compassion begins by empathy with others, when we truly care about their well-being. Compassion is a sympathetic consciousness for the suffering or condition of others, a true understanding and sharing of their pain and emotional distress.

Freedom is the fourth aspect, and freedom means a freedom of mind. Freedom of mind requires practice in being completely open and honest first with ourselves and then with others. Needless to say, freedom might well include a measure of discretion. Another part of freedom is fearlessness. Perhaps fearlessness should come before the other aspects in order to better assimilate them. Fear is the opposite of love and is a byproduct of our egos. Fear is the root cause of hatred, prejudice, and other unwanted thoughts and practices. We don't have to be practicing Buddhists or assume any other label in order to formulate our own beliefs and a unique purpose and path in life, but other religious and cultural principles may serve as a guide for our learning.

Remember, now, that our energies attract similar energies. In physics, the stronger, higher energies also draw and raise lower energies. If we change our thoughts, our countenances, others will be drawn to our considerate, kind, and loving ways. And it just gets better and better.

Laughter is an essential element of our lives and is a beautiful thing. The laughter caused by a humorous anecdote or situation is good for the body, mind, and soul. Laughter even relaxes blood vessels and relieves stress. Laughter can also relax muscles, lower blood pressure, and add up to ten years to our lives. Worry has never solved any problem. For some of us, laughter is much like a big eraser that can make us totally forget about stressful and unwanted thoughts and events in our immediate past and awareness. With a lifestyle in accordance with our beliefs, we can find much more to laugh about and can laugh more often. Human nature says that it is far easier to know love when we are happy than when we are feeling stressed, angry, or fearful. When our awareness of love and beauty grows sufficiently, worry, fear, anger, and stress will begin to disappear.

Have you ever experienced the contagion of someone else's laughter? Laughter is a prelude to joy. For example, when I hear my wife talking with friends and suddenly begin laughing, I too laugh, as I sense her joy, and I become happy for her without ever knowing the context of her conversation. Ever notice that people who laugh often are very easy to be with? Laugh with them, and become more like them.

What would life be like without hugs? History has described how people once used a hand salute as a greeting to show that their primary weapon hand was empty. Sometime later, the handshake served as a common greeting, showing an empty sword hand. The custom of a hug or embrace probably began with family and loved ones, then carried over to business partners or merchant traders, and then evolved to include others. A few weeks ago, while visiting with family and friends, I was introduced to a young man who was also visiting. As he approached me, he extended his right hand to me in greeting. I took his hand and drew him closer to give him a hug. I had thought that it might surprise him, but the surprise was mine. He not only responded with warm embrace, but did so in his Muslim custom by placing his cheek upon mine and then again on my other cheek, and finishing with a light kiss on my cheek. He was truly delighted to learn that I would immediately accept him and his customs. I was made to feel that I was visiting with a dear old friend. A hug can be such a simple gesture with huge rewards! As a very pleasurable experience, a friendly hug with another person of any age can convey affection, happiness, trust, security, openness, fearlessness, empathy, and, of course, love.

Do you know that the electromagnetic field around the heart is nearly fifty times stronger than the similar field surrounding the brain? There are studies that indicate that the human heart has more influence on the brain than the reverse. Those people who work with the human body energy chakras know that each chakra corresponds to differing aspects or issues related to our spiritual growth. It is the heart chakra that deals with the emotional issues of love, hatred, resentment, grief, forgiveness, compassion, and hope. Let's look, then, to those things, those matters of the heart. Let's learn to see love, beauty, and purpose in all things. Surely knowledge, understanding, and compassion will then grow.

# Beauty Surrounds Us

In creating our own reality or changing our existing perception of life's events, it behooves each of us to realize that love and beauty are the essence of our true being. Beauty is the most obvious because of our capability to see and hear the harmony and patterns in nature. Each of us can remember having observed a beautiful, glowing, red sunset. Remember too, a robin's song to greet the dawn? Can you see the silent strength in an old, majestic oak tree? The cognitive experience of beauty does not require any mental thoughts to experience the pleasure or joy in what we've seen or heard. A few years ago, I climbed into the garage rafters to rescue an exhausted hummingbird. This beautiful little creature could not find its way back out of the garage and would soon have perished without cooler air and fluids. A hummingbird weighs less than one-twelfth of an ounce, and I was filled with amazement as this tiny bird sat in the palm of my hand. I held this bird up to the feeder, where it perched to recover. Only recently, while writing this book, I sat outdoors to take a break, wondering what I could say about the love of nature and beauty. Within minutes, a brightly colored bluebird flew down and landed just four feet from me. I knew instantly what this little friend was telling me. Like love and joy, beauty is a function of the soul, and the beauty observed is simply a reflection of the self brought to our mental awareness. Unfortunately, not everyone can or will come to the realization that love and beauty are the ultimate truth of our existence. Even so, your world, your reality, can be a much more wondrous experience just for the change of perception.

The scope of nature is vast and also filled with turbulence, violence, death, and decay in a balanced act. The ever-changing theater of the visible and invisible universe will not always bring us bluebirds, but what we can see is the infinite, beautiful, and very powerful world filled with the intricate, smallest, and most amazing wonders of life forms. A true love of nature is the love of all of creation and the understanding of the interconnectedness of all things, large and small. Whether we are looking at the celestial bodies or a simple wildflower, the beauty and elegance of nature is far beyond the scope of the man-made copies of beauty in art and science. However, when we look for and enjoy beauty everywhere, we begin to see, not only a beauty of those things physical, but also the subtle things, like another's smile, the laughter of children, or the workings of synchronicity, or what we often call coincidence. A good place to begin is with our recognition of the physical, mental, and spiritual beauty within each of us in our human form.

Too many of us in this world are seldom or never happy with our lots in life. Perhaps we have become victims of our own experience and believe that we have been dealt a difficult role in the game of life. At these times, it is really difficult to see much beauty in our world. Many of us have struggled for years with intense, demanding work, oppressive debt, illness, the death of loved ones, and the stress of not knowing why we were destined to struggle so. The emotional and physical stress can begin to take a toll, with resulting poor health, injuries, and surgeries.

It was coincidence that brought me to a children's hospital, where my attitude, my perspective, and my life changed within minutes. It was an epiphany, the sudden awareness that my life could have been much worse and that it was my attitude and perspective that had been permitting me to see my life as only negative events with little beauty. There are now so many reasons to begin and end each day with happiness and gratitude.

Consider what I observed that day: While waiting in the hospital lobby-waiting room, I observed a young boy approaching with his mother. He was bald and ashen-white from treatments, and he walked very slowly. His face appeared expressionless and without hope. His eyes were weary beyond his years. Suddenly, my weakness and infirmity were nothing.

A short time later, a very tiny young girl on small crutches also entered the room.

Her smile and indomitable spirit stood out against her struggles with a crippled, deformed body. Pity quickly faded to empathy, and compassion turned to love. I was thankful—not for my lesser pain, but thankful for the beautiful lessons of love and a new awareness that they brought to me.

# Think and Do the Right Thing

When was the last time that you said or did something stupid and knew immediately that it was harmful or unkind to others? It leaves us with a horrible feeling, knowing what we've done to another being. Once we reach the age of reason at six or seven years of age, we develop what has been called a conscience, to remind us of what is morally good or bad. Of course, some individuals mature without that sense of right and wrong and simply care only about their own welfare. Since the beginning of time, people have been governed by religious commandments, church doctrines, military rule, rule of law, and even the philosophy of Confucianism. In some time periods, these rules were meant simply to maintain an orderly society. The church commandments, designed to regulate morals and conduct in colonial New England, were later referred to as the blue laws, which evolved into some of our present statutes and lawful ordinances. Throughout the evolution of these societal restraints, we have known right from wrongful behavior because of our conscience and our regard for other human beings. As our world becomes more civilized, our collective, universal consciousness and our desire for under-standing, peace, joy, and love also grow. But as we wait and evolve, each of us must take responsibility for our own actions and words and do the right thing. A wise man once said that as we think, so shall we act; and as we think, so shall we become. Consider in all of your thoughts, words, and actions then—is this necessary? Is this thoughtful, kind, compassionate, and worthy of my time? Is it true or a fictional construct of my mind? Do I think kindly of all of my creation?

Over many centuries, numerous poets and philosophers have tried to describe love. We can now find several kinds of love: defined as philos, unconditional, eros, agape, and other labels. Love begins to look like a mental function, to be decided upon and abandoned at will. Love, however, is a realization of the soul, much like beauty, truth, and joy. Many of us find that the sudden onset of love has caused us to lose our senses or become childish or irrational; but love is not a product of our minds. When love finds us deserving and decides to visit, it will come to us when we least expect it.

While en route to self-actualization and a larger transcendent love, we more likely will first be overwhelmed by a love for another person. At this level of experience, the best description of love is the total identification of the self with the beloved. Identification is to the point that the total well-being, welfare, and happiness of the beloved is all that we know, unconditionally. Love then says good-bye to the ego and fear. It is the necessity of the human ego that creates the largest stumbling block to our relationships and to love.

There are hardly words to adequately describe the experience of transcendental love. This acquired state of being is an experience of wonderment or agape, peace, and contentment. When we can arrive at this experience, all other human emotions are balanced, and some, like fear, simply fall away. It is at this level of our human experience that those heartfelt moments that we cherish will then provide the ultimate wisdom of the heart.

By now you must have wondered about *wisdom of the heart.* So, what is this wisdom? Wisdom is the practice of using our knowledge and heartfelt experience in doing what is right and beneficial for others. Wisdom is of no value unless shared, and that raises the question of our purpose for being and for acting. Do you know your purpose in this life on earth? Far too many people simply exist and live day to day, waiting for experience to be brought to them. We are born to this existence for a purpose much more eloquent than to work, play, procreate, and die. Love and beauty are our inheritance and should be shared. Traditional ways of sharing our talents with others have included using our minds, our bodies, and our wealth. These are gifts given us to use with the realization that they do not belong to our true self or being, but are useful, temporary resources for our physical existence. We can use our minds to solve problems, to create possibilities to serve others, and to share with them what we have learned. Examples might include tutoring children, writing, or assisting senior citizens. Likewise, we can use our physical bodies to perform acts of service such as performing errands, household tasks, and volunteer work for others. No matter how much or how little our finances, we should be able to make contributions or otherwise share our wealth with others, beginning with family, friends, and charitable causes. Doing something without ego, for the benefit of others, asks that we look to our skills, our knowledge, and abilities and find ways by which we can enrich the lives of others with love and fulfill our purpose. We can do the right thing.

# The Beloved

Love is like a butterfly. We can chase it only to find it elusive. Yet, if we wait patiently, it will alight upon us.

More than twenty-five years ago, a friend suggested that I attend a local lecture series to hear an interesting speaker. When I ignored this advice, another friend, unknown to the first one, also suggested that I attend the same lecture series. I thought to myself, "What a coincidence—

I *will* go to see and hear what this is all about."

When I arrived and entered the meeting room, I immediately saw the most beautiful woman, seated near the door to greet attendees. Her smile was warm and welcoming, but it was her eyes that suddenly held me in a trance, much like a rabbit caught in the glare of headlights. Love at first sight left me dumbfounded and speechless. I felt that I must know more of this wondrous woman and how it was that I was so captivated. I returned the following day for another lecture, just to see her once more.

She was there again, as if waiting in ambush of my heart and mind (if anything remained of my mind). We then parted ways with me not knowing anything but her name, her smile, her eyes, and my captive heart. Nearly a year and a half went by before I found, by coincidence, the phone number and address of this same lovely woman. Imagine my surprise when I learned that she now lived but one mile from my home. I knew in my heart that the numerous coincidences were part of my longing to know this woman as my wife. Then something magical happened: I sent her a small love note and the next day she agreed to meet me and say hello. I arrived and parked near her car and we began walking toward one another. I had no idea of what I would say or do. Without stopping, she walked into my waiting arms and we shared a soft, memorable first kiss there in the warm May sunshine. There were not words to describe my feelings, but instantly I knew that my purpose in life was to love her unconditionally and without regard to being loved. We were married on the May 2 anniversary of that first kiss and have been together now for more than twenty-four years. Our love continues to grow deeper and more rewarding each and every day of our lives.

Coincidence will bring two people together and, with exquisite timing, will continue to provide the opportunity for love to grow. For most people, the meeting is a two-way physical and emotional interaction. Friendship grows, and romance enriches the communion. The many factors involved in a close, personal, and lifetime relationship usually begin with friendship, trust, affection, compatibility, and desire. Love will grow slowly for some and quickly for others. Some of us will be taken with love at first sight. Friendship, trust, romance and other aspects then will follow. Our path to a transcendental love will likely include our love's focus on a single individual, whether a religious figure or a present-day relationship. So, just who is it that we will call our *beloved*?

When we are completely given to love, the entire universe looks different. The eyes of love see joy in a smile or laughter and see empathy and compassion in another's plight. Hope and passion energize our lives. Just who is the beloved who can cause you to see and feel these things? Examine closely this relationship, as it will surely be one to enrich your very being with experience and the wisdom of the heart.

The love of all creation is certainly admirable, though not always easy. Love of family members and friends seems not to inspire the same passion and commitment as the love for one very special person. Have you ever wondered, What is the difference between the love that you experience with a sibling or a child and the cherished love that you share with another adult? There is only one love, but we share this gift with others at varied levels— hence the names philos, eros, agape, and others to mentally categorize love.

It is intimacy that determines the difference in our various levels of relationships. Consider that intimacy includes two or more people sharing secrets, beliefs, dreams, hopes, values, pain, feelings, and their physical bodies. With our beloved, we share intimacy to a deeper, more enriching level than we would with family, friends, and associates. When we share at this deeper level, we are giving more of ourselves for the benefit and the well-being of the beloved. For those with emotional reservations or doubt, the total sweet surrender to love can cause a feeling of vulnerability. Giving so much of one's self can cause a feeling of risk—the risk of being hurt or the fear of losing something. Contrary to some beliefs, we do not lose our true identity or soul—we find it. This becomes very evident in the shared intimacy of two persons in lovemaking. Passion with only self-gratification denies the opportunity to consider the pleasure and well-being of the beloved before self. Sexual intimacy with our beloved is love's greatest expression of affection and can approach a spiritually transcendent level. It is the deepest level of love's intimacy that will bring us the most rewarding experiences, memories, knowledge, and wisdom of the heart.

Previously, I described a Buddhist principle of fearlessness, and this is perhaps the most important essential aspect of love. Love has no regard for fear, but love is experienced in a direct opposite balance to fear. How many people do you know who love unconditionally, fearlessly, and with joy and complete abandon? To love others unconditionally is to abandon fear and know an overwhelming sense of freedom. Once we have come to experience unconditional love for one person, our world begins to change, and we find that we also love others, without fear of consequence or of being hurt.

Far too many people only love some people, some of the time, and for only some reasons. Most likely, we have all been hurt in one or more of our relationships in life because of our expectations of others. When a loved one does not fulfill our expectations, we can easily succumb to mental exercises of the ego outside the realm of love. Doubt, too, is a cousin to fear, and both are products of the human mind. It is a difficult concept for the ego to accept, but we should understand that others do not hurt our feelings. We hurt our own feelings with doubt, misunderstanding, mistrust, rejection, and fear. We can know that others can only provide the situation, conditions, or stimulus for our conditional, emotional response of feeling hurt and betrayed. Afraid of being emotionally hurt or betrayed again, many people will quite naturally set up barriers and safeguards to protect themselves from added hurt or the risk of loving fearlessly again.

For many of us, forgiveness has been an obstacle, not because we wanted to remember forever those persons who caused us pain, but because we believed that we, as humans, did not have the moral authority or the right to pass judgment upon others. One day, it suddenly came to me that forgiveness is simply the act of letting go of the *remembering* of the painful experience or the person associated with it. Any former belief I had held that there was pain or hurt feelings was something I had inflicted upon myself—a creation of my mind.

Many of us who are fearful and cautious because of a love lost will look to our pets or children for unconditional love without expectations. If only we could know what we have lost in not looking to a forgiving, healing heart and another chance to love with complete abandon. We must learn to view the ache in our hearts as part of being vibrantly alive, and be thankful for the experience. We should know, too, that the fear of loss is a separate mental construct. We must see the heart and the mind as separate. It is only to the depth of our love that we can experience the depth of the heartache. These heartfelt experiences are among those that bring us to the wisdom of the heart.

I am reminded of the words of the philosopher Kahlil Gibran, when he wrote that love requires nothing and neither takes or gives anything but love. Love will not possess anything nor will love be possessed.

She lay sleeping so peacefully while I sat quietly and watched her breathing. Such beauty! I longed to touch her and to trace the outline of her lips and face with my fingertip, but feared waking her. Could she know the love I felt at this moment? In time, she would know. After all, our granddaughter was but three weeks old.

# Get a Life

Much of this book is devoted to the importance of changing and directing our life experiences and, thereby, increasing our awareness and expanding our consciousness. We can choose to expose ourselves to an increased knowledge and the understanding that leads to wisdom. We can consider, too, that knowledge is simply part of our awareness of facts or information. In suggesting how we can change our lives, I have talked about our lives as mental and physical experiences. The reality is that only our egoistic mind calls this existence a life. Our consciousness, or true self, is life. If we are to change our mental-physical existence, we must know the difference between that of *being* and that of *thinking*. We can do many things to acquire knowledge, understanding, and even wisdom; but we cannot, with our ego, cause ourselves to arrive at a spiritual awakening. It simply happens. It may happen only when we submit to the will of a greater creative power.

Only when we discover and understand the difference between the ego mind-self and our true being or self, can we fully identify with our true being. Once we know the essence of our true being, we begin to experience our love of self and know the importance of love and beauty. *This is the spiritual awakening.* We can, then, also know the usefulness of the ego element of the mind as a tool for accomplishing things. This awareness allows us to truly get a life—a new life with meaning and purpose. To learn to first love ourselves allows us to forever change our lives, change our behaviors, improve our health, and open our hearts to others.

A great source of experiential knowledge may be found through meditation. Meditation means many things to people, depending upon their orientation and/or their imagination and depth of commitment. For some, meditation is simply finding the time and location to treat themselves to a "time-out" for relaxing and introspection, much like a biofeed-back experience. Others consider meditation a discipline of prayer and devotion.

Taken to deeper levels, meditation can concentrate our attention and our awareness on our thoughts and expose the talking ego. This concentration can cause the loss of sensation of our physical bodies and five physical senses. For many, the repetition of a word mantra is often used to reign in the constant chattering of the mind. I say "good luck" with that one, as the human mind is capable of at least nine separate and simultaneous channels of communication. Many more of us simply channel or concentrate our thoughts in a very powerful way of prayerful gratitude. The key to this meditation is to set aside our egos and replace them with humility.

Often this is called mindfulness meditation. This type of meditation actually changes brain serotonin, hormones, and other bodily functions in a positive, rewarding way. It is then that our conscious awareness can travel to other realms of consciousness within ourselves. When we ask for assistance in our inner travels, the experiences can also come to us from our superconsciousness during our sleep periods, when the body is functioning on autopilot. I mention this, because lucid sleep experiences show that meditation, or going within ourselves, does not have to be a discipline of sitting uncomfortably with our eyes closed. Some physical routines and disciplines are necessary and helpful for beginners to learn to hold their awareness in a concentrated, directed manner. However, once we learn the routine of directing the chattering mind, we can sense our true being. Then, with grace and with practice, meditation can include all of our daily activities. With loving thoughts, humility, and gratitude for everything given us, we can make meditation our way of life, a state of being in a raised consciousness. Our meditation should then also include our acknowledgment of a higher creative force to which we can direct our requests for assistance in creating other events in our changing reality.

Many people are afraid of meditation, fearing that they must give up their identity or control of their rational mind. Quite the reverse is true, and the benefits can begin to manifest physically, intellectually, and spiritually.

There are several levels of consciousness, and each of us is functioning at one or more of these levels simultaneously. The various levels of consciousness are not stratified with exact boundaries separating each level, but instead, overlap slightly. The third level, or causal level, is often referred to as the universal mind. This is the source of the power and life of the human mind. The first level, of course, is that of the physical plane of our existence. Consider that a person sitting at his or her desk on the physical level can use the causal-level mind power to write a classic musical piece with information gathered from the second-level astral realm. Beyond the first level, or gross physical realm, is the realm or state of being that is more commonly referred to as the astral realm. On the astral realm is a separate region known as the Akashic records, where one can find all information about anything and everything that ever existed, including our thought forms. Lessons and information sought and received in experiences at this realm are without words or language, but are instead received as instant knowledge with a complete understanding. This is also our first stop for transition and a review of our lives after death on the physical plane. For many of us, it appears much like a quiet, peaceful college campus. It appears this way to me, because I have imagined and believed it to be so, much in the manner that your vision of this phenomenon will be just what you believe it to be or what you have heard suggested by others. The same experiences of instant knowledge may also be received in our physical, wakeful state of consciousness as well. These are the "ah-hah" moments we experience when something previously elusive is suddenly known and completely understood by us.

In a previous chapter, I described a secret knowledge, passed through the ages, that allows us to seek and to have many things. The use of this practice also allows us to ask for assistance and to find answers to our many questions within the human body-temple. There are, then, higher realms of consciousness for exploration and knowledge, but there are not words to begin to describe these experiences, except to say that we don't go anywhere else in

the universe for these travels, but access
them from within ourselves. Your experiences will differ from mine, as we create
our own unique realities from countless
possibilities.

Matthew 22:14 notes that, "Many are
called, but few are chosen." Have you
been chosen? Perhaps you now have more
questions than answers or a continued
longing for meaningful transformation of
your life and your purpose on earth. In
our evolving world, each of us is obligated
to contribute to an ever-increasing spiritual awareness and consciousness. Join the
many thousands of people who have
found a personal spiritual awakening.
Find the real you, the silent listener and
spiritual being. This, alone, will change
your life forever. Secondly, take the time

to look closely at your basic beliefs and the course of your present life experience. To change your future to include heartfelt meaning and purpose, you must first believe that you can. Then, decide what it is that you want most and begin creating the reality that you wish to experience. I sincerely hope that love and beauty will bring to you a continued spiritual awakening to share with others.

Thank you for your interest in the wisdom of the heart and for allowing me to share some of my thoughts with you. As for the heartbroken police officer at the beginning of this book—he has found much, much more than just answers to his many questions.

978-0-595-51436-6
0-595-51436-7